Little reflections

E.M Gow

BookLeaf Publishing

Presentation by *BookLeaf Publishing*

Web: www.bookleafpub.com

E-mail: info@bookleafpub.com

ISBN: 978-93-95890-07-6

First edition 2022

For my husband and children, for always believing in me and making me think about things more deeply than I could ever have imagined

The watcher

I sit at the edge of the flat concrete roof.
Five storeys. High enough to jump off.
A hundred and thirty-five steep steps up.
I counted. The thud of shoes on concrete and
panted breaths echoed loudly in the
stairwell as I climbed each one.
Up here, the wind is sharp enough to
slice through you, piercing the warm
marrow in your bones with its chill.
You can see for miles, right to the edge of the
horizon,
sharp-tipped with pink and purple.
I watch people scurry in the streets below.
Their frantic, constant movement a ballet
amidst the beaming glare
of headlights and streetlamps,
as they skirt across the surface of glistening
puddles and tiptoe past
cracks in the pavements
with superstitious precision.
Honking horns and expletives yelled out
of car windows, the rumble of trains deep
underground, provide the melody they dance to.
Silently, I watch on —unseen, unknown—
my legs dangling over the edge, my hands

latched on to the cold, grey stone.
Knuckles white and holding fast.

No medals here

He falls to the floor, exhausted.
His forehead is crusted with sweat-dried salt.
His tongue darts out, lizard-quick,
raking moisture over the ragged and raw
skin of his lips before the sun steals it away.
Blood soaks through his socks and into
the torn leather of his shoes. His feet
are cushioned by clusters of blisters, small
balloons of pain so fierce he has to hold
his breath as they strike the ground. He cannot
look at them. Will not.
At night he dreams of water, of the cool balm
of morning dew, of droplets studding the
gossamer
of spiderwebs and pooling in the pits of petals.
Yet the rains do not come, and the miles
keep stretching out in front of him,
time rendered elastic.
He brushes the dirt and specks of gravel
out of the raw skin on his knees, gets
unsteadily to his feet, and starts walking.

Festival

The streets team with throngs of people.
Swarms of tourists descending on jugglers
and panpipe players. Coins are thrown
into buckets and hats as payment.
On every street, bins overflow with
bags of dog dirt and burger wrappers.
Polystyrene chip boxes have been
torn into pieces by the gulls like
bits of confetti scattered in the wind.
Show flyers carpet the pavements,
dreams trodden underfoot until they are mush.

Bar

She deftly weaves a path through the sea of
people,
squeezing past gaggles of groups and amorous
couples,
somehow miraculously managing to avoid
jostling elbows and spilling drinks or tripping
over bags left unattended on the beer-sodden
floor.
She is sluggish now, the adrenaline she felt
from the crowd has long since worn off
and the bone-deep ache of weariness has set in.
A roar swells up from the bar but she refuses
to get caught up in the melee of backslaps
and bear-hugs exploding all around her.
She piles glasses up on trays balancing each one
with gravity-defying skill then
carries them aloft, raising trophies of her own.

The right reason to write

When people ask why I keep writing,
I am not sure how to answer.
I am told I must want to see my name in print.
Is that what I want?
Sure you do, they insist.
Everyone wants that, don't they?
I love the process, sliding into images
and dissolving in phrases.
It's just like chemistry. Or baking.
You have to gets the measurements right;
tweaking combinations and
weighing words against each other
until the right words are placed in the right order
and the perfect balance is achieved.
Even if no one else ever reads them.
That is more than enough reason to write.

Clean

Sometimes I wish
I could take my brain right
out of my head
and rinse it under a tap,
scrubbing away the murky anxious
thoughts and grimy, lingering
streaks of self-doubt
in cool, clear water.
Then pop it back in,
all shiny and sparkly and
working properly again.

Porthole

It was hard to see through the dirty glass.
I scrubbed the cuff of my sleeve over it,
smearing the grime away
until there was a small clearing.
I peered through it like a Dickensian orphan
staring at a fat roast on a pub table,
caught in that delicate space between
being scared to death and feeling exhilarated
and more alive than ever, waiting eagerly
to see what would emerge from the gloom.

to talk or not

9

He saw a flash of unhappiness dart across her
face.
The sight of it was unexpected,
he thought it had been going so well.
He wanted to ask what was wrong, if
there was anything he could do
to make it better, whatever it was.
Then he thought better of it and went
and made a cup of tea instead.

Bad Gateway

I wish I could busy myself with
chores or other simple tasks to
quieten my frazzled, frantic mind
while waiting for an email reply to appear
or for a website to load.
I wish I could step away from the F5 button,
stop dragging my thumb down the screen
forcing it to refresh, or from opening extra tabs,
clogging the bandwidth in the hope
of sneaking in through a crack.
I wish I was patient.

Stasis

For a moment I was frozen—
an insect trapped in sap—
waiting for a cartoon lightbulb
to appear above my head
and everything to snap
sharply into focus.
But the right path didn't unfurl
magically in front of me
and there was no guiding angel
on my shoulder, no neon arrow
pointing me in the right direction.
The only way to go was forward,
and face any monsters there may
be, lurking in the shadows, head-on.

Twilight

The sky was darkening quickly
and in the heady gloam the
night mist began to fall,
enveloping her in its cool, damp velvet.
The sudden change from day to eve
chilled the air. Her breath
spurted out in plumes —dragon-like—
as she navigated her way,
the cheerful orange hue
of streetlights guiding her home.

Hard reset

He talked automatically, without thought,
knowing what he was saying was
garbled and nowhere near
what he actually wanted to say.
He looked at his feet and tried to slow
down, focussing on the scuffed leather
and the frayed laces that had been
knotted back together more times
than he cared to count.
Calmer now, he took a deep breath and,
raising his eyes to meet theirs, began again.

Daydreamers

They lay on their backs and stared at the sky.
There was enough blue to make a sailor
a pair of trousers she said, with a smile,
remembering the grandmother who had
said the very same thing long ago,
as she had nestled on her knee.
They formed animals and buildings
out of clouds, cities created from droplets
and vapour borne on distant gusts of wind,
until the sun slunk quietly beyond
the edge of the horizon, and the
distant peal of bells beckoned them home.

Cafe morning

I look up from my mug of tea
and take in the scene unfolding in front of me.
Harried mothers clutch oat milk lattes
in their hands while their unimpressed, red-faced
progeny chew on bran muffins they dream
were pancakes covered in Nutella instead.
Businessmen order americanos with extra shots
made from the strongest beans, barely slowing
their pace to before they exit efficiently,
the door swinging wildly in their wake.
Everyone is so busy, there is so much
to do, so many places to be arrived at.
I was once like them, chasing brief moments of
free time in jam-packed schedules.
Now I am grateful to be outside of those storms,
where it is quiet and still and
I can take my time enjoying the singular
pleasure found in simple mugs of tea.

Different paths

It was only four in the morning
but the day already felt alive
and ripe with possibilities.
She lay in the snug cocoon
of her duvet and watched as drops
of rain raced each other
to the bottom of the window.
She was always surprised by the different
paths they took, the most obvious path
–straight down– was never taken.
She decided right then she would
be like a raindrop and enjoy
the random twists and turns of
her journey, rather than hurtling down
directly and never taking the
time and space to look around.

August

The days were long and frantic
and filled with constant noise,
the drone of workplace chatter a dull,
persistent buzz, like an angry bluebottle
bashing off a windowpane.
Tempers frayed at the edges in the
humid midday air and movements
slowed to a near standstill
in the haze of the heat.
Yet the memories of those times
were never more evocative or fond.
They remain dreamlike, now, never
tainted with the bitterness of regret
or the sting of missed opportunities.

Hypnopompic

When I wake up it is dark outside
and, for a moment, I forget who I am.
I rub my eyes and the rooms swims
slowly into focus but seems unfamiliar.
It looks very nice, but I do not know it yet.
I stretch out in the bed, swooping
my limbs over the comforting cool areas
of the cotton sheets that my
sleep-heavy body has not yet warmed
and revel in the delicious freedom afforded by
the brief few moments before my
memory kicks back into action
where I could be anyone, anywhere.

Bad timing

A flash of red catches my eye
and I turn quickly, too fast,
losing my balance. My heel
catches on a crack in the
pavement and I wobble
precariously —my arms wind-milling
uselessly in the air— until I am
able to steady myself.
By then whatever it was
is long gone and
the thought of what it
might have been accompanies
me the whole journey home.

Writer's block

He sat at a desk behind a typewriter
and let his fingers ghost along the keys.
He wondered how many letters or works
of fiction were written at this very place.
He felt all the history of this humble tool,
could almost hear the frantic clack-clack
of the keys piercing inky ribbon into parchment
as inspiration took hold, or feel the roller
ratcheting each leaf precisely into place.
He hasn't been inspired to write for a
long time, but now the words itch to
flow out of his fingertips and
burst their way into existence, tales
of love and loss from a time long since past.

Sensing endings

It is often said that starting
is the hardest part of anything.
That once you start you will find
a rhythm, a groove and everything falls
into place like it should.
I think endings are much scarier,
the space beyond them is empty
and vast and begging to be filled
with something, anything.
The unknowable is terrifying.
I'll happily start a thousand poems or
a hundred journeys. Crossing starting
lines does not trouble me,
but placing the all-important,
final full stop always will.

Close and yet far

In an instant she was on her feet
and moving across the room at a pace
that surprised everyone, especially her.
Despite her haste, the vase itself seemed
to be falling in slow-motion, defying gravity
as it inched ever nearer the cold slate floor.
She dipped her chest like an athlete straining
to burst through the ribbon at the end of a race,
her fingers stretching out hopefully into the air,
grasping for a prize just slightly out of reach.

www.ingramcontent.com/pod-product-compliance
Lightning Source LLC
LaVergne TN
LVHW010023200726
843495LV00015B/1904